Lantau Trail

The Chinese ha[ve] Lantau. They call it Tai Yue Shan: Big Isla[nd] isle in the SAR's archipelago, Lantau's m[ountains] wider and its valleys more secluded than those of Hong Kong Island. And until the relatively recent arrival of Hong Kong's replacement airport at Chek Lap Kok, together with the adjoining satellite town of Tung Chung, it had – despite its great size – fewer inhabitants than tiny Cheung Chau. Here, you can still lose yourself.

People have made their homes on these sheltered shores since Neolithic times. The first islanders were probably members of the Yue, a vanished seafaring people. Rock carvings at Shek Pik and a mysterious stone circle at Fan Lau may be attributed to them. Chinese settlers came from the north during the Han Dynasty, and left their pottery and coinage behind. The island remained an imperial backwater until the British arrived two millennia later, with the exception of a brief period in the 13th century when the last rulers of the Sung Dynasty took refuge on Lantau from the invading Mongols. Two temples to Hau Wong honour a courtier who did his utmost to protect the boy emperors.

Surviving saltpans and lime kilns, which represent ancient rural industries, can be seen at Tai O and Yi Long. Qing-dynasty forts still stand on coastal bluffs. Relics of the colonial period include two obelisks which mark the limit of then-British waters.

The 70 km Lantau Trail takes in many of these sights. Starting from Silvermine Bay, it strikes westwards into the central uplands, crossing two major peaks in succession and passing high above Hong Kong's longest beach. It visits the Big Buddha at Po Lin and descends to the stilt village of Tai O. And then, after circling the serene wilderness of the southwest, it loops back to follow the southern coastline back to its beginning.

Over half the island has been protected since the 1970s as country park – a lucky circumstance when you consider the recent urbanisation of its northern shore. In the midst of an increasingly overdeveloped Pearl River Delta, Lantau and its waters remain a haven for indigenous wildlife.

Lantau Trail

The only circular route among the major trails, the Lantau Trail rings the southern half of the SAR's largest island. You have new choices when heading out to Lantau for a hike. The traditional sailing from Central to Mui Wo still operates, but is now joined by

the MTR connection to Tung Chung. The new skyrail up to Ngong Ping is a good alternative to the bus for those sections which start or finish near the Big Buddha. And yet solitude is still easy to find on this mountainous isle.

	Stage	Route
	Stage ❶ **Mui Wo 梅窩**	Mui Wo 梅窩 > Nam Shan 南山
	Stage ❷ **Sunset Peak 大東山**	Nam Shan 南山 > Pak Kung Au 伯公坳
	Stage ❸ **Lantau Peak 鳳凰山**	Pak Kung Au 伯公坳 > Ngong Ping 昂坪
	Stage ❹ **Ngong Ping 昂坪**	Ngong Ping 昂坪 > Sham Wat Road 深屈道
	Stage ❺ **Keung Shan 羗山**	Sham Wat Road 深屈道 > Man Cheung Po 萬丈布
	Stage ❻ **Tai O 大澳**	Man Cheung Po 萬丈布 > Tai O 大澳
	Stage ❼ **Fan Lau 分流**	Tai O 大澳 > Kau Ling Chung 狗嶺涌
	Stage ❽ **Tai Long Wan 大浪灣**	Kau Ling Chung 狗嶺涌 > Shek Pik 石壁
	Stage ❾ **Shek Pik 石壁**	Shek Pik 石壁 > Shui Hau 水口
	Stage ❿ **Tong Fuk 塘福**	Shui Hau 水口 > Tung Chung Road 東涌道
	Stage ⓫ **Cheung Sha 長沙**	Tung Chung Road 東涌道 > Pui O 貝澳
	Stage ⓬ **Pak Fu Tin 白富田**	Pui O 貝澳 > Mui Wo 梅窩

Distance in km	Duration	Challenge
2.5	0.75	Easy rambling
6.5	2.75	Strenuous hiking
4.5	2.25	Strenuous hiking
4.0	1.25	A fairly challenging walk
7.5	2.75	A fairly challenging walk
2.5	1.00	A fairly challenging walk
10.5	3.00	Strenuous hiking
5.5	1.50	A fairly challenging walk
6.5	2.00	Easy rambling
6.5	2.00	Easy rambling
4.5	1.25	Easy rambling
9.0	3.00	A fairly challenging walk

total **70**

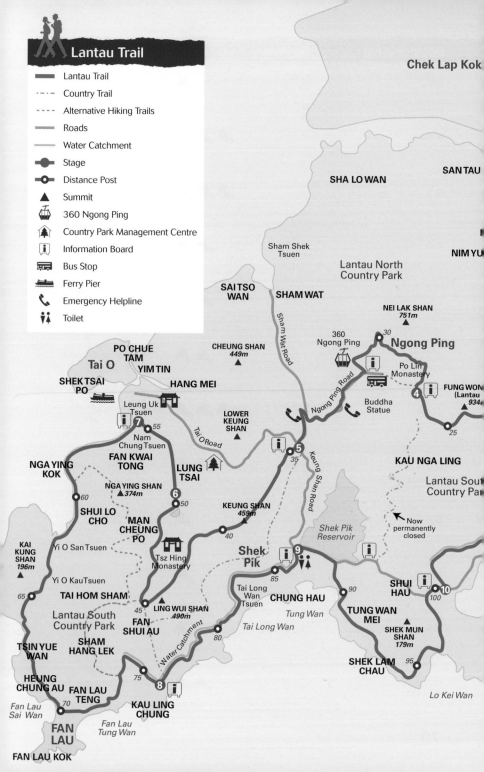

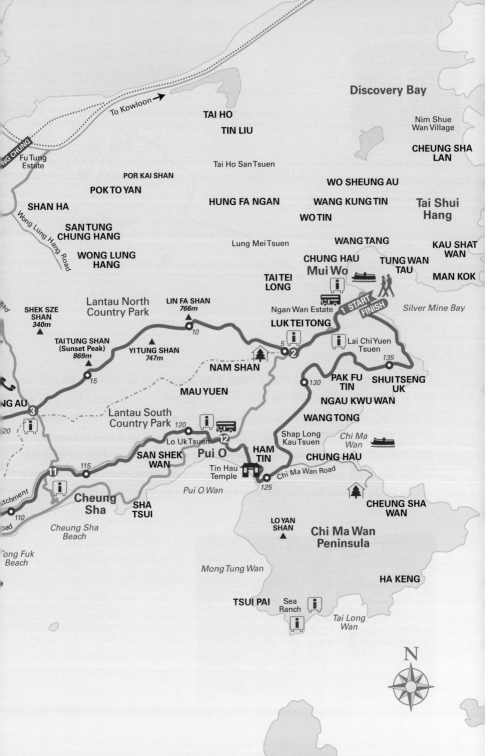

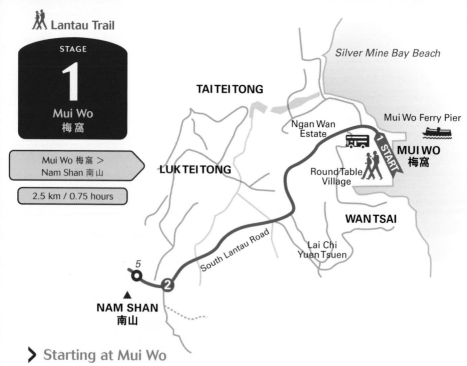

人 Lantau Trail

STAGE
1
Mui Wo
梅窩

Mui Wo 梅窩 >
Nam Shan 南山

2.5 km / 0.75 hours

TAI TEI TONG

LUK TEI TONG

Silver Mine Bay Beach

Ngan Wan
Estate

Mui Wo Ferry Pier

MUI WO
梅窩

Round Table
Village

WAN TSAI

Lai Chi
Yuen Tsuen

South Lantau Road

5

2

NAM SHAN
南山

> ### Starting at Mui Wo

Take the ferry to Mui Wo (Plum Nest, also known as Silvermine Bay) from Pier 6 in Central. Departures are more frequent at weekends but you will rarely wait longer than 45 minutes. The journey takes just under an hour on the slower, more enjoyable triple-deck ferries, which are equipped with refreshment counters and open-air sundecks. Other ferries may be faster, but their windows are sealed, packing you into the equivalent of a rather large fridge, butting its way through an extremely bumpy crossing.

Striped tree lizard in nature's disguise

Mui Wo appeared in the history books just once, when the last boy emperors of the Sung dynasty were forced to stop over in the bay in 1277, while fleeing from Kublai Khan's advancing Mongols. No evidence of their travelling court remains.

A journey of 70 km begins with the first step

Leaving the ferry pier, turn right and walk past the massed ranks of bicycles towards the traffic roundabout, where you'll see the Silvermine Bay branch of HSBC. The South Lantau Road starts here, at the yellow Nam Shan marker, and Stage 1 follows this uphill. The road is restricted to vehicles with permits, and other than buses and blue Lantau taxis, traffic is light.

You pass the Lantau South Division Police Station, perched on a hilltop surveying Mui Wo. Further on, gaps in the roadside trees allow good views of the wide, flat valley, dotted with villages, which provide popular habitations for commuters. Here on the right two trees stand guard over marker *L002*. Markers *L003* & *L004* follow in quick succession. A short climb brings you up to Nam Shan.

An alternative route, which avoids the main road, runs up from Luk Tei Tong in the Silvermine Valley. Take the coastal promenade from the ferry pier to the Silver River estuary, and then follow the signs to Luk Tei Tong. From there an old village path of stone slabs ascends to Nam Shan.

Lantau Trail

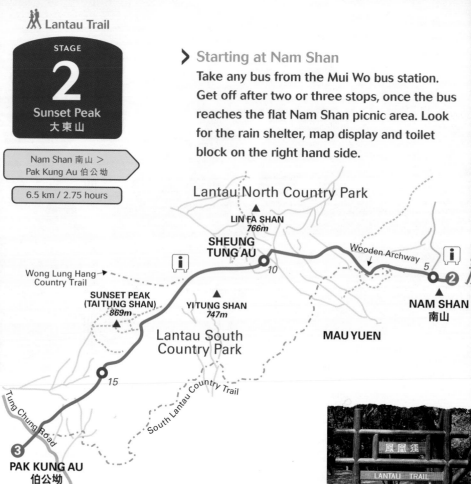

STAGE 2
Sunset Peak
大東山

Nam Shan 南山 >
Pak Kung Au 伯公坳

6.5 km / 2.75 hours

> ## Starting at Nam Shan
> Take any bus from the Mui Wo bus station. Get off after two or three stops, once the bus reaches the flat Nam Shan picnic area. Look for the rain shelter, map display and toilet block on the right hand side.

Lantau North Country Park

LIN FA SHAN
766m

SHEUNG TUNG AU

Wooden Archway

Wong Lung Hang → Country Trail

SUNSET PEAK (TAI TUNG SHAN)
869m

YI TUNG SHAN
747m

Lantau South Country Park

MAU YUEN

NAM SHAN
南山

South Lantau Country Trail

Tung Chung Road

PAK KUNG AU
伯公坳

The Lantau Trail starts in earnest at the wooden archway by *L005*. Here you will find a pleasant area shaded by trees with rest pavilion, benches, BBQ pits, camping facilities, a public toilet and cool drink vending machines which accept cash but offer nothing in return and much prefer your Octopus card, provided you give the apparatus a solid thump. Pass underneath the archway and

L005 Stone-stepped gateway into distant hills

climb the steps beyond. At first following a lovely walk along which various trees at great public expense are labelled and described, the trail crosses a little-used whitewashed helipad to leave the tree cover behind.

Up and along a sun-dappled pathway – but not on the seat of your pants

L008 Hiking higher, Mui Wo recedes

Accessible eyrie: the path to Sunset Peak is clear

Feeling insignificant on Sunset Peak

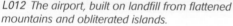

L012 The airport, built on landfill from flattened mountains and obliterated islands.

Rising steeply up the lower slopes of Sunset Peak, the path ambles on over old stone steps and is partially tree covered until it reaches *L008*, where we are exposed to sun and wind. It's not long before expansive views of Mui Wo and the islands of the western harbour open up on your right. Further south, the broad sweep of Pui O beach points towards Chi Ma Wan. If you have brought binoculars, look closely for the wild water buffalo which inhabit the sandy estuary.

The path is covered in pine needles and rubble, providing a pleasant natural crunch underfoot, and is steep in places; but tall grasses catch the sunlight to lift your spirits along with your feet. At the pass, *L010*, turn left

L010 Up the north face of Sunset Peak in companionship

to cross over onto the northern face of Sunset Peak, the second-highest point on Lantau. You'll pass a welcome single-plank bench and several rock pools with rushing streams – the latter depending on the season. Ignore the turning for Wong Lung Hang (Yellow Dragon Stream), a valley which descends in the direction of Tung Chung.

Turning a corner, you find before you the wide plateau between the twin summits of Sunset Peak. On a clear day at *L012*, as Barbra Streisand predicts, you'll be offered splendid views of the airport with its accompanying satellite town of Tung Chung from this vantage point. On your right a Country Trail mapboard points the way to Wong Lung Hang Road and Tung Chung. Our trail

L013 Stone huts, like an obsolete mountain kingdom, dot the high ridge

Bunkers on boulders: shelter against the upland climate

L013 Dressed as Mandarins, Christian missionaries on R&R in the 30s

however bears left. Two dozen stone huts at *L013*, dot the ridge like the remains of some obsolete mountain kingdom. Built between the wars as a holiday retreat for missionaries working in China, these huts may be rented by making advance bookings. All food and drink must be carried up the hill with you. As late as the 1970s, porters were available for hire in Mui Wo; the sons of those "sherpas" are probably now currency traders or village house landlords.

A swimming pool, formed by a dammed stream, exists just south of the huts, tempting in warm weather but only practical if there has been recent rain. Unflappable wild cattle graze the plateau, calmly standing their ground when approached.

.013 Blessed with ample rainfall, the mountain community prospered

Lantau Mountain Camp: chalets on the plateau have stories to reveal

L015 *Heading towards the northeast ridge of Lantau Peak*

Pui O sheltered by the buttresses of southern Lantau

L015 Lantau Peak dominates the skyline

The trail leads west up impressive boulder stairs but bypasses the actual summit of Sunset Peak (Great Eastern Mountain in Chinese), which may tempt you to make a short detour to the top. Hidden until you pass *L015*, the great bulk of Lantau Peak dominates the sky to the west.

From here on it's all downhill, on a handsome boulder path edged with shrubs and young trees. The descent is tough on the legs, but the views are spectacular: the south coast far below fringed by Cheung Sha, Hong Kong's longest beach, and offshore, the uninhabited Soko Islands, navigation points for hydrofoils racing towards Macau.

Stage 2 ends at Pak Kung Au, a pass named for the traditional Earth spirits, which protect passes, fords and villages. The Tung Chung Road runs north-south over and across this pass, and buses can be flagged down for both Mui Wo and Tung Chung, but only at actual bus stops. *L018* Picnic areas with covered pavilions have been built on both sides of the road.

Patterns to perplex predators

This winding route was laid by the British army in 1966 to provide access to the then-isolated village of Tung Chung, but it now leads to the ever-growing new town beside the airport that preserves the name but nothing of the character of the historic settlement it replaces. Massive roadworks have been completed to broaden the existing single track into a highway — literally paving the way for further urbanisation of Lantau's southern coastline.

Travel writer P.H.M. Jones wrote in 1969: "Private cars cannot cross to Lantao yet, but the Hongkong and Yaumati Ferry Co. is thinking of starting a vehicular ferry service to Silver Mine Bay. Thus it may soon be possible to sit in endless traffic jams on Lantao on weekend afternoons, risking heat-stroke and asphyxia, just as in the mainland New Territories." It's unlikely that he could have foreseen the impending bridge to Macau, and the heavy commercial traffic that will bring to this once unspoilt island.

Lantau Trail

STAGE

3

Lantau Peak
鳳凰山

Pak Kung Au 伯公坳 >
Ngong Ping 昂坪

4.5 km / 2.25 hours

> ## Starting at Pak Kung Au

Again take any bus from Mui Wo bound for Tung Chung or the airport, and alight when you reach Pak Kung Au, at the road's highest point. Conversely, you can take any bus from Tung Chung bound for southern Lantau, and get off at the same spot. After undergoing extensive reconstruction the new Tung Chung Road is now almost a national highway. Buses and taxis are that much more frequent.

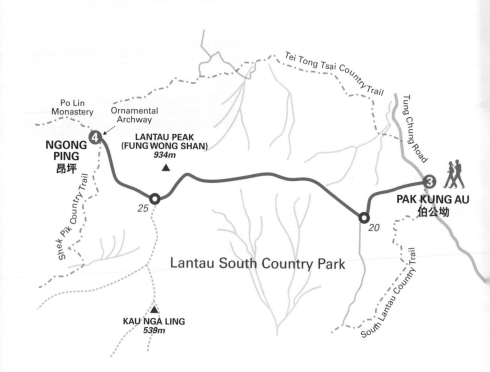

Picnic areas welcome hikers on both sides of the highway

Two trails converge here: the Lantau Trail, with all its ups and downs, and the much easier South Lantau Country Trail, which sticks to a level contour. Our way ahead is challenging: Lantau Peak looms above, and the only way is up.

At *L018*, a great stone pathway climbs dramatically into the mists, inviting speculation as to what mystical Shangri-La may await beyond. When weather conditions allow, such reveries are dispelled by spectacular realities as the sharp ridge walk reveals simultaneous views of both north and south Lantau. Since the opening of the airport on Chek Lap Kok, visibility to the north has deteriorated markedly, although on occasional clear days you

The road ahead for the further urbanisation of Lantau

L020 *The way ahead is clear – though unshaded*

can still distinguish the pointed outline of Castle Peak, near Tuen Mun. Here a new pavilion offers views north over Chek Lap Kok, and adjacent is a memorial plaque to a helicopter crew who crashed in 2003 while on a rescue mission.

The rocky summit of Lantau Peak (or Phoenix Mountain) at *L024*, is the second highest point in Hong Kong. Here one is provided with a 'temporary refuge' in case of unexpected deteriorating weather. Stay for a while in this rarefied atmosphere to appreciate the ranges of folded hills spreading all around. Many hikers spend the night at either Po Lin Monastery at the nearby youth hostel, in order to reach Lantau Peak by sunrise.

L023 Outdoor exercise: better than step classes

At *L020* one can but smile wryly at the bold pronouncement of the Corporate Afforestation Scheme, which proclaims that 'this woodland was established by Cathay Pacific Airways'. One wonders what happened to the promised woodland.

A spectacular stone-staircase, laid on a scale which suggests it could have been lifted from the pages of Gulliver's Travels, forms an impressive descent but takes its toll on hikers' knees. At *L027*, newly installed benches survey the madding crowd below, attending the Sutra Garden, temple eaves, parking lots, cable car pylons, their tour groups ordered into formations by guides with loud hailers – all surveyed in calm repose by the Great Buddha.

The trail forks at *L028*: the path straight ahead descended steeply down spurs through lush vegetation towards Shek Pik Reservoir. But no longer! Our immediate target however, is Po Lin, so we take the right-hand turn.

Sunday solitude – short of the summit

L025 The distant but serene Buddha revives illusions of a more distant Shangri-La

The sight of the giant bronze Buddha, silhouetted beside assorted temples and monastery buildings, briefly revives that belief in Shangri-La — until you spot the countless tourists who have chosen to arrive either by public transport or cable car.

As you reach the Ngong Ping plateau, an ornamental archway marks the end of Stage 3. Walk straight ahead to the Po Lin (Precious Lotus) Monastery, focusing on thoughts of the absolute that transcend clicking cameras and amplified chatter, and you will find bodily if not spiritual refreshment, settling if you must for the convenience of buses to other points on Lantau.

L024 Temporary refuge in foul weather

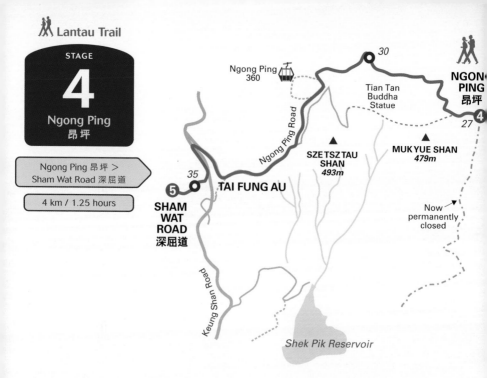

Lantau Trail

STAGE 4 Ngong Ping 昂坪

Ngong Ping 昂坪 >
Sham Wat Road 深屈道

4 km / 1.25 hours

> ## Starting at Ngong Ping

Take bus No. 23 from Tung Chung or bus No. 2 from Mui Wo, bound
for Po Lin. Be warned that at weekends these are not only extremely
crowded, but also charge twice the weekday fare. The arduous climb to
the Ngong Ping (Lofty and Flat) plateau leaves their engines gasping.
A more peaceful (though not inexpensive) alternative is the new cable car
service, which departs from beside Tung Chung MTR station. Be prepared
for long queues of weekend vacationers headed in the same direction.

Aim for the serene Buddha and, keeping the statue on your right, follow the
signs for the youth hostel, the Tea Garden Café, the Sutra Garden, and the
Lantau Trail to find your way to the archway near marker *L027*. However,
one no longer heads downhill along the western slopes of Lantau Peak to
commence Stage 4.

The Rhododendron bushes, the wooded valley resplendent with all
possible shades of green, and resonant with birdsong, chirping insects and
cascading, thirst-quenching water, are no longer accessible. The joys of

L027 Severe soil erosion has permanently closed the trail between L027 and L035

hiking in the shade of dense forest, free from the intrusion of cement paths and unnecessary iron railings, have now been permanently barred from the Lantau Trail. Here the force of nature has intervened to divert the course of what was one of this footpath's most favoured stretches. Inclement weather and excessive monsoon rainfall caused severe soil erosion, exacerbated by landslides which deeply scarred the slopes of Lantau Peak and resulted in the closure of this segment of the trail and many secondary hiking paths in the vicinity.

The Buddha surveys his holy hilltop domain

A nun's story

Sutra verses, mountain slopes

Near the archway beside the Sutra Garden is the relocated marker *L027*. The adjacent mapboard is clear in its directions to the realigned Lantau Trail, which now diverts us through the trees behind the monastery along the 'Wisdom Path'.

At the T-junction we cross over the North-South Tung Chung/Ngong Ping country path and proceed up stone steps into the greenery. Here the path is wide, clay-packed and markers *L028, 029 & 030* make their appearance. En route, wooden benches offer views of the Tian Tan Buddha, seated serenely on a lotus base with a Ngong Ping View Compass detailing the ever-expanding commercial development in the valley below.

Downhill the Trail touches on another T-junction, this time with the country path from Tung Chung which leads to the upper station of the 360˚ cable car. We bear left on an uneven stone and cement track which is distinctly unpleasant to hike on, and lies directly under the flight

L028 Cable cars convey camera-toting 'pilgrims'

L028 *The divine image towers serenely above the weekend multitude*

Thirst-quenching summer falls

path of the overhead gondolas. This section soon ends at a third T-junction with a concrete service road. Bear right and find your way through the main, commercial Ngong Ping Village Boulevard. The trail is signposted. By-passing the tourist shops the trail reaches Ngong Ping Road. Bear right again and head downhill along the congested roadway laden with taxis and fume-belching buses. The trail terminates at its junction with Keung Shan Road, by the watershed between Tai O and Shek Pik Reservoir. Conveniently located here is a bus stop. To return to the city take either bus No.11 to Tung Chung or bus Nos. 1 & 2 to Mui Wo.

Unless shopping for tourist trinkets is on your Lantau Trail agenda, we recommend you avoid this commercial segment of the rerouted trail. Instead, as you leave the archway at marker *L027*, proceed straight ahead on the obvious and only path towards the Great Buddha, passing on the way the Tea Garden Café for a bowl of noodles or a soft drink and the much used public toilet facility a little further on. Once in the main plaza head out along Ngong Ping Road where markers *L032, 033* & *034* appear on the right hand pavement, skirting the crowd and shopping complex to arrive at the junction with Keung Shan Road.

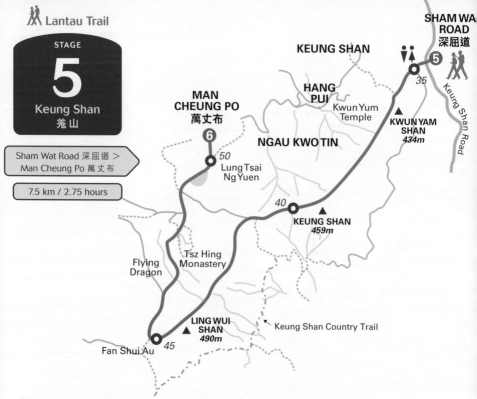

❭ Starting at Sham Wat Road

Board any bus bound for Tai O or Ngong Ping. Alight at the first stop after the junction with Tai O Road, and walk back a short distance. Stage 5 commences directly at the intersection of Sham Wat and Keung Shan Road. Mount a few steps to the trail archway with picnic tables and a shelter pavilion at *L035*.

Striking immediately uphill on a handsome boulder path, you soon enjoy views of the many monasteries and nunneries in the Keung Shan Valley. It's a peaceful spot suited to meditation. One might well reflect upon the effort and ingenuity that went into placing each of these stones, some weighing tons, to form this impressive stairway. Climbing higher, the trail skirts the summit of Kwun Yam Shan, named after the Buddhist goddess of mercy, and then bears right towards the desolate mountains that make up this far southwest corner of Lantau. *L037*, appears directly on the crest of the hill adjacent to a lone tree.

Rolling hills and ridgeway

L037 Filled to capacity, Shek Pik Reservoir lies serenely in the valley

The way ahead is clear: the footpath cuts through low grass, keeping to the spine of the ridge all the way. The soft, rolling hills are devoid of trees, except for the high, narrow valleys which provide refuge from the upland winds. Shek Pik Reservoir lies serenely in the valley to our left.

The next major summit at 459 metres is Keung Shan, or Ginger Mountain, just past *L039*. We are now high above the South China Sea, looking out beyond the Sokos to islands in Guangdong Province. Herds of wild cattle frequent even remote spots such as this.

At the crossroads, take the uphill path. The golden roof tiles of Tsz Hing Monastery appear below. At *L041*, take the left-hand path heading uphill. From *L042*, for the next kilometre it's moderately steep hiking to the summit

Multiple monasteries at Keung Shan

Over the top

of the windy 490-metre peak of Ling Wui Shan, with expansive views in all directions. The path forks at Fan Shui Au. The beaches of Fan Lau lie far to the south. At *L045*, head in the direction of Man Cheung Po. We turn right into the lee of the hill to enjoy serene downhill hiking on twisting dirt paths. On the way down, glancing over your right shoulder, watch out for the flying dragon sculpture.

Cross a small dam, cracked and leaking, with lilies flowering in the pools that remain and then at *L046* follow the sign to Man Cheung Po and the austere green-roofed Tsz Hing Monastery on the hillside above, which dominates this silent upland valley. Water from the dam joins other tributaries, which eventually cascade over ledges to form Lantau's most spectacular series of waterfalls. At *L049*, turn right onto a narrower, more natural path interspersed with concrete steps. The trail continues across long-abandoned farmlands, the sounds of frogs and crickets accompanying a pleasant rush of water.

Stage 5 comes to an end at Lung Tsai Ng Yuen, a somewhat neglected country villa built many years ago by a Buddhist businessman exiled from Shanghai. Set in landscaped grounds with colourful pagodas, elegant pavilions and stands of bamboo, this charming retreat is nominally open to the public, who are too often disappointed on finding it closed. If the sole watchman is on duty, soft drinks at $10 a can are on offer but not chilled, as the place has no electricity and carrying ice cubes from Tai O is not a proposition. In any case, you can walk out onto the dam and admire the ornamental zigzag bridge, which crosses the lotus-filled pond.

From here your nearest access to public transport is via the path downhill, taking the first right-hand turning. This path soon joins a country parks service road which links with Tai O Road. Buses travel from here to points east. Or simply carry on to Stage 6, which will take you to Tai O. We continue straight ahead. From *L051* it's pleasant hiking on natural clay paths through tunnels of greenery, passing on the way the sometimes grandiose and always strategically located feng shui grave sites of venerable local ancestors.

Delicate duet: a pair of Glassy-tiger butterflies

L050 The deserted retreat of Lung Tsai Ng Yuen

Lantau Trail

STAGE
6
Tai O
大澳

Man Cheung Po 萬丈布 >
Tai O 大澳

2.5 km / 1 hour

TAI O 7
大澳

Disused
Salt Pans

Leung Uk
Tsuen

San
Tsuen

Tai O Road

55

▲ **TSIM FUNG SHAN**
339m

MAN CHEUNG PO 6
萬丈布

Tai O: water, water everywhere

❯ Starting at Man Cheung Po

This short section, which begins at a rather remote spot, is usually walked as a continuation of Stage 5. You can, however, reach it by taking any bus bound for Tai O, and alighting on the descent through the Keung Shan Valley after you see a ceremonial gateway on the left. A peaceful country park road ambles alongside a catchwater, passing a rural nunnery, until the turning you seek appears on your left. There are in fact two paths up through the greenery; the first is overgrown and often blocked by fallen bamboo.

Water-bowed mauve blossom

L052 Beyond this point it's a welcome cruise downhill

The trail runs gently downhill from *L050*, near the villa at Lung Tsai Ng Yuen, keeping to the east side of a hill with views over the Keung Shan monasteries. The coastal plain of Tai O is our destination, and it can be seen ahead for much of the way, preceded by its disused saltpans (following spread). Here at *L052* the trail is pleasantly tree covered. On the way one encounters signs of serious landslips and soil erosion, much of the rocks spilling over our path.

Shortly you reach the sleepy village of Leung Uk (Leung's House) on the southern fringe of the saltpans. Head in the direction of the children's playground, and keep this on your left. Some of the pans have been reclaimed for use as sports pitches while others lie filled with shallow seawater. Mangroves are being planted here as compensation for those lost in the construction of Chek Lap Kok.

To reach the bus station at Tai O, follow the new road which cuts directly across to the town. Buses depart for Tung Chung and Mui Wo.

If you have some time on your hands, it's worth taking a look at Tai O, or at least stopping for refreshments. The hand-operated rope ferry has unfortunately been replaced by a less old-world drawbridge over the creek, but if you cross this and turn right onto Kat Hing Back Street, you can take a pleasant walk past tin-roofed stilt houses to the Yeung Hau temple behind the town. Dedicated to the Marquis Yeung, who rendered great service to the Sung boy emperors during their brief sojourn on Lantau, this temple presents an unrivalled waterside prospect.

L052 Landslips deeply scarred the trail on its approaches to Tai O

Abandoned salt pans border Tai O, Lantau's unique stilt settlement

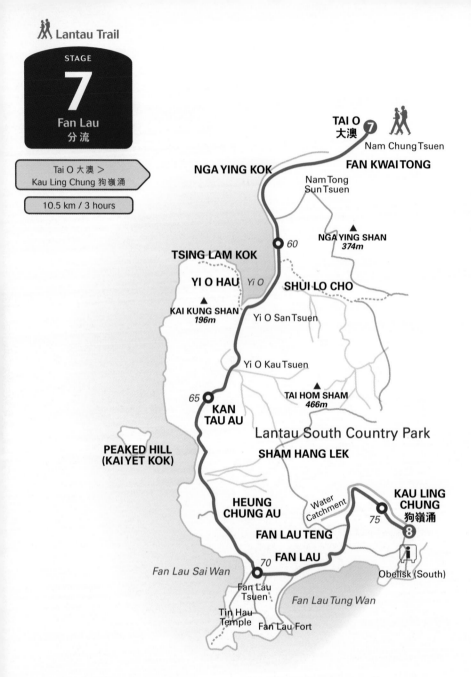

Lantau Trail

Tai O 大澳 >
Kau Ling Chung 狗嶺涌

10.5 km / 3 hours

TAI O
大澳 ⑦

Nam Chung Tsuen

NGA YING KOK

FAN KWAI TONG

Nam Tong
Sun Tsuen

NGA YING SHAN
374m

TSING LAM KOK

YI O HAU *Yi O*

SHUI LO CHO

60

KAI KUNG SHAN
196m

Yi O San Tsuen

Yi O Kau Tsuen

TAI HOM SHAM
466m

65

KAN TAU AU

Lantau South Country Park

**PEAKED HILL
(KAI YET KOK)**

SHAM HANG LEK

KAU LING CHUNG
狗嶺涌
⑧

HEUNG CHUNG AU

Water Catchment

75

FAN LAU TENG

FAN LAU

Obelisk (South)

Fan Lau Sai Wan

70

Fan Lau Tsuen

Fan Lau Tung Wan

Tin Hau Temple

Fan Lau Fort

> Starting at Tai O

Tai O used to be regarded as the unofficial 'capital' of Lantau, a title it has since relinquished to Silvermine Bay and Tung Chung in succession. In recent years it has even lost its irregular ferry connection to Central. To reach it, you must take lengthy bus rides from either Tung Chung or Mui Wo – try to avoid the 45-minute detours certain journeys make through the back streets of Mui Wo and down to the detention centre at Shek Pik – or catch one of the weekend ferries (which also call at Sha Lo Wan) from Tung Chung or Tuen Mun.

Leave the town and head south in the direction of Nam Chung Tsuen, traversing old saltpans to discover the start of Stage 7. Due to severe landslips, the trail has recently taken a few twists and turns. At the time of going to press, this short segment had not yet been clearly defined. Pass the pink-tiled houses and head towards what used to be the venerated village tree standing as a memorial to the former marker *L055* that is no longer

At Yi O, coloured pennants flutter in the breeze

there. Broadly speaking, the path is coastal, with hills on one side and sea on the other. Pass at first through a jumble of village houses, restaurants, a toilet facility, and you will find, at *L056*, the Island District Council shelter with yellow seats resembling a bus stop. But don't expect a bus here any time soon. It's not long before all traces of human habitation are left behind. The sea stretches away to the western horizon. Macau must be out there somewhere.

To placate absentee landowners who fenced off areas of the existing trail ahead, an optional segment was introduced which commences at *L058*. It branches off to the left up stone steps and heads over the crest of Nga Ying Shan via Man Cheung Po to meet the original trail again at *L074* near Kau Ling Chung.

L057 *Fallow and shallow: the deserted lands around Yi O Bay*

Happily the older route remains passable so we continue on as before. A short distance further we arrive at the pleasant, shaded, two-tiered Nga Ying Kok rest stop, with its continuous flow of fresh stream water. Opposite, secluded in the trees, is a toilet facility.

At the bay of Yi O, a lonely seaside temple watches over shallow waters, its coloured pennants fluttering in the breeze. Yi O was once inhabited by farmers, but over time the muddy Pearl River silted up their bay, leaving their jetties standing on dry land.

The cement path ends suddenly at *L062* and you are required to take to the shore; but not for long, since the path then makes a sharp left turn to plunge into humid undergrowth, leading you across soggy leaves, fallen branches, rocks and mossy tree trunks. You may stumble upon the ruins of substantial stone walls, and wonder what might have driven the farmers of yore to build to such dimensions.

This part of the Lantau Trail was fenced off by absentee villagers in 2001, who claimed that it trespassed on their property. The incident cast a worrying shadow over the legality of all major hiking trails. Since then, it

Stepping stones amidst autumn leaves

Silent reminder of once-thriving villages

has been possible to walk this section with no obstructions beyond the occasional fallen tree, but the matter seems to have been resolved since the introduction of the alternative route.

The path ascends gradually through a thickly vegetated valley. Though the trail is overgrown on both sides, especially at the end of summer just prior to the hiking season, the rock-pounding surf is a constant acoustic reminder of the sea's proximity. Large village houses near the pass slowly crumble into the surrounding jungle. The first tangible evidence of the continuing validity of this segment of the trail is marker *L065* that appears adjacent to an electric pylon. The view south is wonderful: empty bays and offshore islands. As it reaches the coast, the path skirts a wide beach which, at low tide, connects the offshore isle of Peaked Hill (or Chicken Wing Point) to the mainland. The western end of this beach is populated by hundreds of large crabs.

L070 Des res: detached house, sea view, needs a touch of paint. Would suit family of rice farmers

Continuing south, the trail rises slightly and again heads inland to pass the very basic Tsin Yue Wan campsite at *L068*. Then there's a steady descent to Fan Lau, Lantau's southernmost extremity. The large but abandoned village straddles a sand bar linking what used to be an offshore island to the bulk of Lantau. As a result it is flanked, front and back, by two golden sandy beaches. Fan Lau means Division of Flows, a reference to the waters on either side of this headland. It is here that the brown muddy currents of the Pearl River Estuary meet the deep blue of the South China Sea.

At *L070* an impressive ancestral hall faces west, its tall doors hanging open but adorned with newly affixed door gods. The long-abandoned village school is attended only by spiders. The remaining population of Fan Lau consists of two ancient villagers, both of whom sell cold drinks from their houses. Village mongrels are noisy but toothless, and friendly to hikers.

A detour to the imperial Chinese fort on the headland (opposite) can be made by climbing the stone steps from the southern end of the beach. The fort has been a ruin for more than 150 years but it's easy to see how Ming or Qing soldiers could have used it as an advance warning station. A nearby Tin Hau temple stands in splendid isolation on its own beach.

The trail moves on through the village, where deserted houses (previous spread) are steadily enveloped by creepers. From here it's again pleasant hiking on a natural earth path. Great trees spread their shade over roofs that have collapsed under the weight of time. Passing above Fan Lau's eastern beach, the trail mounts the hillside on sun-baked stones, with effective and unostentatious chain fence providing a barrier between hikers and the cliffs below.

Beneath lies the photogenic beach of Kau Ling Chung, backed by a green lagoon and dramatic hills. The trail forges on to join a waterworks catchment road, but

Modern motion from a venerable viewpoint

Fan Lau Fort: Qing-dynasty stronghold

L072 Crescent bay below the fort

Lush countryside for all to explore

you can make the descent to the bay by following a rough track leading off to the right.

On a spur above the beach, reached by taking a footpath from the catchment, a Royal Navy obelisk erected some time after 1898 marks the furthest extent of what at that time had just become British waters, under the 99-year lease of the New Territories which expired in 1997.

The treaty was obviously somewhat flawed, since it left a large portion of Lantau sticking out into international waters. Junk crews from China made use of this anomaly right up until 1997, landing, among other things, vegetables for sale at Tai O, in the full knowledge that they could escape the not-so-long arm of the Royal Hong Kong Police by simply jumping back on their boats and hovering six feet offshore.

At *L074* a newer path heads back to Tai O via Man Cheung Po. This route was introduced as a fallback option in case the AFCD was unable to resolve the land dispute at Yi O, and is now appearing on updated mapboards.

Stage 7 ends at the catchment above Kau Ling Chung. However, your only way back to the road is to follow the new path to Tai O or continue on to Stage 8.

Rugged Kau Ling Chung coastline

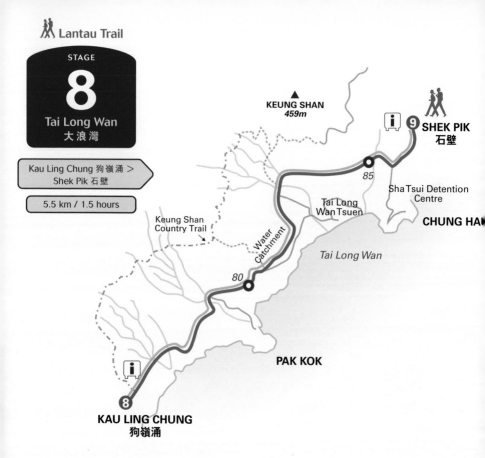

Lantau Trail

STAGE 8
Tai Long Wan
大浪灣

Kau Ling Chung 狗嶺涌 >
Shek Pik 石壁

5.5 km / 1.5 hours

KEUNG SHAN
459m

SHEK PIK
石壁

85

Sha Tsui Detention
Centre

CHUNG HA

Tai Long
Wan Tsuen

Keung Shan
Country Trail

Water
Catchment

Tai Long Wan

80

PAK KOK

KAU LING CHUNG
狗嶺涌

> ## Starting at Kau Ling Chung

This section is usually walked as a continuation of Stage 7. Or you can reach it by following Stage 5 over Ling Wui Shan and turning left at Fan Shui Au to descend south.

This is an easy stroll along a catchwater road for its entire length, shaded by tall trees much of the way.

The last part of the hike on stone steps emerges at the catchment between *L073* and *L074*. From here until the end of this section it's a steady plod along the service road, which closely skirts the catchment for its entire length. Occasional tracks branch off downhill to secluded sandy bays.

Watch out for snakes which enjoy the heat of the paved road. No human settlements are seen until Tai Long Wan village appears on its beach far below. This prospect is a reminder that we are approaching the giant Shek Pik reservoir, with the prison and detention centre at its base.

The dam was built in 1963, and after completion the valley below Ngong Ping was flooded to create the reservoir. It was the largest in Hong Kong at the time. Chinese copper coins dating back to the 8th century were discovered during construction, posing something of a puzzle since Lantau was then supposedly inhabited only by aboriginal tribes.

There are five-star toilet facilities at the corner of Wang Pui and Keung Shan Roads. The bus lay-by is across the road next to marker *L087* on the near side of the dam.

A juvenile, red-necked Keelback.
The most commonly seen snake on the Lantau hike

Shek Pik 石壁 >
Shui Hau 水口

6.5 km / 2 hours

❯ Starting at Shek Pik

Buses heading towards Tai O or Ngong Ping all have to cross the long expanse of the Shek Pik dam. Get off at its far end to start your hike.

Walking back across the dam, you enjoy an outstanding view of the flanks of Lantau Peak descending to the waters of the reservoir. The Big Buddha watches benignly over you from his platform on the Ngong Ping plateau, and the auspicious *L088* makes its appearance exactly halfway across the dam wall.

Upon reaching the eastern end of the dam, cross the Shek Pik Reservoir Road to take the smaller lane southwards, following the yellow Lau Tau Trail marker for Shui Hau via Lo Kei Wan. Walk behind the beach towards the Red Cross youth camp. The trail turns left here into the greenery along a handsomely constructed stone footpath which evolves into a sand trail with occasional stone steps, lined with groves of fresh, young bamboo.

L088 Blossoms and the Buddha

Fresh water streams after seasonal rains

L089 *The reservoir rarely overflows*

Shoulder-high shrubs and blossoming trees provide nectar for humming bees but little shade for the hiker. The path ascends steeply on natural and man-made stone steps to peak on the ridgeline overlooking the beach. Shelter is achieved further on, as the path descends into thicker forest closer to sea level. There are exceptionally pleasant hiking conditions between *L090* and *L095*, where the calming effect of tree cover, rocks, sand and fallen leaves is augmented by the sound of the rhythmic tide below.

Steady steps on solid stones

Skirting the quiet strand at Lo Kei Wan (Bamboo Basket Bay, but unofficially known in English as Cowpat Beach), the path strikes uphill by way of a grand stone staircase of manageable and evenly spaced treads, evidently set in place by engineers with hiker's empathy. An altar honouring the sifu of stonemasons would not be out of place here.

The trail joins a service road. Turn left to complete the final stretch.

A herd of Lantau cattle, no doubt responsible for the cowpats seen earlier, graze on the turf nearby. Shortly the main South Lantau Road is joined at the village of Shui Hau (Water Mouth). This spot is named for the watercourses which empty here into the muddy bay, home to endangered species such as the horseshoe crab.

The village shop is a little way off to the right. Drag the shopkeeper away from her TVB drama to supply you with drinks and nibbles. The village rents holiday rooms to trippers at weekends, but on weekdays it's so quiet that cattle often settle down in the middle of the road.

This section of the trail ends at *L100*, with its mapboard a little further down the road. Buses can be waved down from the stop near here to take you back to Mui Wo or Tung Chung.

L096 Cowpat Beach: surf, sand and salt air — but mind your footing

L096 Weekenders share the shade

L096 Weekenders share the shade

Lantau Trail

STAGE 10
Tong Fuk 塘福

Shui Hau 水口 >
Tung Chung Road 東涌道

6.5 km / 2 hours

Lantau South
Country Park

South Lantau Country Trail

Water Catchment

110

South Lantau Road

Lower Cheung
Sha Beach

Ma Po Ping
Prison

TONG FUK

105

Tong Fuk Beach

Tong Fuk
Centre

Tong Fuk Miu Wan

100

10

SHUI HAU
水口

TUNG
CHUNG
ROAD
東涌

11

> ## Starting at Shui Hau
Board any bus bound for Tai O or
Ngong Ping, and alight just
before Shui Hau village. Don't
confuse this with Tong Fuk
village, which appears earlier
and looks identical. Walk back in
the direction from which you just
came, passing the public toilets.
The trail starts at a mapboard on
the inland side of the road.

*Indigenous to Hong Kong – the elongated
rostrum Lantern Fly*

Heading directly uphill in the direction of Lantau Peak, the path meets the main South Lantau catchwater between markers *L101* and *L102* at an elevation of 100 metres, and turns right to follow a level course. This and the following stage are also cycle tracks. Ma Po Ping Prison, at the intersection at *L105*, lies below the trail at Tong Fuk, Lantau being the Hong Kong equivalent of Australia's Botany Bay; one of the government's chosen locations to detain convicts.

Alert, intent and ready...

Relaxed hiking along the Catchment Trail

Mimosas line the catchment, interspersed with barbecue areas. The catchwater is often dry and becomes a trap for small animals and even snakes. Should you encounter a serpent, your best course is to stay still and let it escape: I have twice come face to face on Lantau with Burmese pythons, but in each case the gigantic snake was given a respectfully wide berth and allowed to slither away into the undergrowth.

Between *L109* and *L110* you are offered cinemascope views of Cheung Sha beach through the trees. A steep path leads up to the left to conquer Lantau Peak, but our trail follows a level contour to meet the former Tung Chung Road at *L113*. Should you wish to exit the hike at this point, be warned that public transport is no longer available here on what was the Tung Chung Road. Here you have two choices. Either walk downhill to enjoy a swim at Cheung Sha, and return to your point of departure later in the day by bus, or proceed along the catchment to reach stage 11.

Slippery encounter with a Green Bamboo Snake

Watercourse over rugged rock

Lantau Trail

STAGE 11
Cheung Sha
長沙

Tung Chung Road 東涌道 >
Pui O 貝澳

4.5 km / 4.25 hours

South Lantau Country Trail

120

Pui
San
Ts

PUI
貝沙

Lo Uk
Tsuen

WA
TS

Pui O Beach

Water Catchment

South Lantau Road

SAN SHEK WAN

YWCA Youth
Camp

Cheung Sha
Sheung Tsuen

Acacia
Villa

Pui O Wan

Tung Chung Road

TUNG CHUNG
ROAD
東涌道 11

115

CHEUNG
SHA

Cheung Sha
Ha Tsuen

Upper Cheung Sha
Beach

> Starting at Tung Chung Road

From Mui Wo take any bus going to Tung Chung and alight at Tong Fuk.
Then head directly uphill in the direction of Lantau Peak. Find your way
to the picnic area at *L113*, look for the catchment service road on the
southern side of the pass and point yourself east.

116 The South Lantau Island expressway slices the Trail

The trail follows a level route along the well-shaded waterworks track, traversing the southern foothills of Sunset Peak. At *L115*, the recently completed Tung Chung – South Lantau Island Road superway slices across the Lantau Trail overhead. However the road engineers were considerate to a point. This intersection offers an escape route to either Tung Chung or Mui Wo, which you attain by traversing the underpass, adjacent to the mapboard and mounting the stairs to the highway's surface for conveniently located bus stops heading in either direction.

The catchwater finally terminates at *L119*, and the welcome sand-and-stone path immediately begins to lose altitude, descending towards Pui O (Shell Bay) village. As you turn right at *L120*, its attractively curved beach can be seen beyond the village houses in the foreground. The wild, green Chi Ma Wan peninsula serves as backdrop to the view.

Walk left along the main road through the village to the end of this section, marked by a police post. The straggling settlement has several bus stops, transport being available to all other points on Lantau.

L119 Buffalo beach and the village of Pui O

👣 Lantau Trail

STAGE 12
Pak Fu Tin
白富田

Pui O 貝澳 >
Mui Wo 梅窩

9 km / 3 hours

MUI WO FERRY PIER
梅窩碼頭
FINISH

Sewage Treatment Works

Lai Chi Yuen Tsuen

South Lantau Road

135

130

PAK FU TIN

NGAU KWU WAN

SHUI TSENG WAN

WANG TONG

PUI O
貝澳 12

Ham Tin San Tsuen

Shap Long Kau Tsuen

Chi Ma Wan

SHAP LONG

Pui O Beach

125

Chi Ma Wan Road

❯ Starting at Pui O

To get to the starting point, take any bus from Mui Wo – it's just a few stops away – or a $30 taxi ride. Alight in the middle of the unkempt Pui O village, opposite the Police Reporting Centre and just before the school. Stage 12 starts at a side road which leads off to the left.

alanced burden: bamboo baskets

Holiday home in spring surroundings

Placid buffaloes languish in the surrounding mud pools

To be assured that you are headed in the right direction marker *L122* asserts itself directly next to the CLP sub-station.

Following the newly completed road between what were once productive paddy fields, but now lie fallow, you cross a bridge to reach the village of Ham Tin. Restaurants under venerable

L124 Seafront temple of Pui O

village trees are open for business on weekends. Here companies maintain holiday flats for staff and in more recent times modern, western-style three-storey buildings have proliferated, but the location is not particularly inviting. Further on, following the winding river, the setting improves: the village temple at *L124*, overlooks the estuary with Pui O beach on the opposite side. Fauna to occupy your attention range from mudskippers and red-clawed crabs to a herd of feral (but non-aggressive) water buffalo that inhabit the mud pools in the area.

Turn inland here on the Chi Ma Wan Road. Rising gently to a point where the opposite coast becomes visible, the trail makes a sharp left turn at *L126*, to start the first serious climb of this section. It's steep going for the

L123 High tide of the Pui O estuary

next 500 metres, then after *L128* eases off somewhat with the hill ascent ahead. Commencing under tree cover, the path soon emerges onto low scrubland. The highest point is marked by a clump of trees embracing a police radio installation. From here you can look down to catch glimpses of the occasional inter-island ferry calling in at Chi Ma Wan (Sesame Bay) to the southeast.

Hiking and biking: mountain bikers share the trail

L134 Last legs on the last stretch home

Dropping into cool, forested valleys, the trail meets a service road at *L133*, but then immediately turns left, up a brief and clearly signposted flight of steps, back downhill into the greenery. Venturing out across grassy upland towards the eastern cape of this coast, it bypasses the tiny bays below, dotted with abandoned farmhouses. On the way you come across the Pak Fu Tin campsite, well equipped with running water, barbecue pits and toilet facilities.

Turn left at the tree-planting site. A rest pavilion cum rain shelter is at your disposal at *L135*, but since you're almost home and dry, there is no need to procrastinate any longer. As you walk the last section, lined recently with not insubstantial metal tubing, courtesy of the Water Authority, Silvermine Bay becomes visible ahead, sheltered in the late afternoon light by its surrounding range of hills. And look! There's the ferry you were planning to catch. But don't worry, another will be calling in soon.

The path descends abruptly to, yes, you guessed it, Mui Wo Ferry Pier Road at *L139*. The *China Bear*, a clutter of restaurants, the pier and ferries to usher you home in air-conditioned comfort, are just five minutes further along the waterfront.

Inter-island ferry – Hong Kong bound

Captivating coastline: there's always another bay, and another beach, just over the next line of hills